KIDPRENEUR

Genius Ways For Kids
To Pay Their Way Through College.

By Dallas Crilley

Manufactured in the United States of America

For information, please contact:

Brown Books Publishing Group

16200 North Dallas Parkway, Suite 170

Dallas, Texas 75248

www.brownbooks.com

972-381-0009

A New Era in Publishing™

ISBN-13: 978-1-934812-25-9

ISBN-10: 1-934812-25-0

LCCN: 2008931518

1 2 3 4 5 6 7 8 9 10

Table of Contents

Table of Contents

Table of Contents

Acknowledgments

Dad, you're first—you've been here throughout the entire project, and I'm just surprised that we've taken this little idea from Quiznos all the way to the finish line. We went through with one of our genius ideas finally. Next up is the Do Nothing Club.

Mom, thanks for listening to my stories and for just being my mom—I couldn't have done it without you!

Sarah, taking midnight runs to Burger King is always a blast, and I couldn't ask for a better sister.

Victoria, you rock. Thanks for believing in me. You can have your Harry Potter back now.

Thanks to **Gabe** and **Jordan**, because I know you'd be mad if I didn't put you in here.

Thank you to all of my **teachers** and **role models** who helped to shape me into who I am today—I owe you all everything.

Thanks to my publisher, **Milli Brown**, of **Brown Books Publishing Group**—without you this book wouldn't have been possible. You never treated me like a kid. My illustrator, **Bill Young**, was amazing! Bill, you've got skills. Thanks to **all at Brown Books**—you've all made my first publishing experience special.

And most of all, thanks to all of **the amazing kids in this book** who had the chutzpah to stop waiting for something to happen and decided to go out and make a difference.

Introduction

Most kids have had a job at some point in their life, whether it's dog walking, lawn mowing, or babysitting. However, it takes a special kind of kid to turn those jobs from just another way to make burger money into a successful business. We live in a great country that gives us all kinds of opportunities, and it's a crime that so many kids with great ideas don't take advantage of that fact. For some reason, there's this imaginary number—eighteen—that kids seem to think is the age when they can start making money. So instead of going out and following through with their ideas, they sit at home and play video games instead.

Kidpreneur is a book filled with true stories of kids who've earned a small fortune from a homegrown business, proving that running a successful business is actually child's play. This book is for all kids and parents who believe that you don't need to be an adult to make something of yourself.

Chapter One

OPPORTUNITY KNOCKS

Recipe for Success!

The Story...

Joseph Semprevivo was just nine years old when he was diagnosed with juvenile diabetes. When he was eleven years old, his parents decided to open an ice cream shop, and Joseph began making ice cream that he couldn't even eat because of his condition. Obviously, that was a problem—you try working around ice cream all day without being able to eat it!

However, Joseph had the idea to make sugar-free ice cream for other diabetics and health conscious people. After much experimentation, it worked; he had invented the first sugar-free ice cream. He started selling it to local stores.

Four years later, when Joseph was fifteen, he switched to sugar-free cookies instead of ice cream because he couldn't take the ice cream to school as a snack. Joseph's Lite Cookies was born.

Now, Joseph's Lite Cookies is in almost 140,000 stores in fifty different countries. It's the best selling sugar-free cookie in the United States.

The Secret...

This is a great example of finding a need and acting on it. Joseph was diabetic, and at the time there were very few diabetic-friendly desserts out there. He didn't wait until he was eighteen.

Also, he used the resources that were available to him—his parents owned an ice cream store, and he realized he could use that to his advantage.

Now It's Your Turn...

Look around for something that you know and that is true to you—something you're passionate about. If you see a need in your community, act on it. Getting started is the hardest part. Once you go through with it, what doesn't kill you only makes you stronger. Every mistake and success becomes a learning experience, and soon you'll know the taste of sweet, sweet success.

"Success usually comes to those who are too busy to be looking for it."

-Henry David Thoreau

Catching the Snitch:

Cashing in on a Craze!

The Story...

Emerson Spartz was just another bored twelve-year-old with too much time on his hands when he started MuggleNet, a Harry Potter fan site. He never dreamed his little Web site would cast such a spell on Potter fans all over the planet.

MuggleNet is now the largest and most popular Harry Potter fan site, receiving more than thirty million visits a month. The site is filled with book and movie reviews, trivia, downloads, and discussion boards. Emerson's young voice and way of looking at the Potter craze struck a chord with kids.

Advertisers flock to his site and his MuggleShop does a booming business in Harry Potter merchandise. In fact, Emerson is now nineteen years old and paying his way through business school at the University of Notre Dame. Somehow he finds a way to balance school and media appearances, all while running a company that has grown to over 120 volunteers and paid employees.

The Secret...

Emerson followed his dream. Maybe it's because when you're twelve years old you don't know any better, but I believe that if adults would listen to their hearts instead of their heads sometimes, they would be a lot happier in the end. Instead of sitting at home playing video games, Emerson jumped on his idea of making a Web site. He didn't wait to put his plan into action. In fact, his Web site wouldn't be as successful if he had! Other fan sites would have been created, and he would have missed out.

He cashed in on a craze. 1999 was a breakthrough year for the Harry Potter series. It was getting tons of media, and all Emerson did was build on the buzz and give fans what they wanted: a Web site that had not only the latest information on the series but a place to hang out.

Now It's Your Turn...

This is an easy story to learn from, folks. There is nothing restricting you from following your dreams until you're eighteen. What are you waiting for? Go out and do it! For some reason, we live in a society where there's some crazy, unwritten rule that you have be an adult to start making money. That's outrageous! Childhood is a time when you do some of your best dreaming. I'm sure many great ideas are tossed aside because someone thinks they're "too young" to put them into action. If you have a great idea brewing in the cauldron of your mind, act on it! The results will be magical.

" Lack of money is the root of all evil. "

-George Bernard Shaw

Just Plane Genius!

The Story...

For as long as Lance Winslow could remember he'd been fascinated by planes. When Lance was just twelve, his father who was an airplane pilot suggested that he make a little extra money cleaning planes at his local airport in Camarillo, California. Lance would vacuum and polish the airplanes, making ten dollars per plane. In no time at all, he was cleaning thirty-five planes a week. Do the math. $350 a week isn't bad for a twelve-year-old.

While hanging around the airport all the time, Lance would hear people talk. It was mostly adult stuff—business, taxes, that kind of thing. Then one day he heard a guy talking about wanting to sell a plane and remembered another man who wanted to buy one. So Lance did what came naturally: he introduced the two to each other, and his plane brokering business was born.

"One guy said he'd buy me lunch because I'd sold his airplane," Lance says. "That's when I decided I would start charging 2 percent." Now keep in mind, he was only fourteen and just going into high school.

"I sold one and made $240. Then I sold another and made $500." It wasn't long before Lance's business took flight.

Before retiring at the age of forty, he started running several successful businesses, doing everything from mobile oil changes to truck washing. Even though Lance is now retired, he's never forgotten the lessons he learned by hanging around the hangar.

The Secret...

Sometimes money can be found in things and jobs no one else wants to do. Cleaning an airplane certainly isn't glamorous, but running to the bank with pockets full of cash every week is.

Lance was observant. There are probably a lot of people, even adults, that could overhear conversations from different people wanting to buy or sell something and not be able to put the two together.

Now It's Your Turn...

Lance had the self-confidence to ignore anyone who told him he couldn't do it. Every time, he thought, "Watch me!"

He says that the secret to success is never giving up. You'll make mistakes along the way, but the lessons you learn now will help you in any future business that you operate. Lance points out that being a child entrepreneur can be a great marketing advantage. Anything a kid does is instantly cute. The Girl Scouts sell countless cookies each year to adults who may not even like cookies. "Beginning early also gives you the practice and understanding of how to succeed," Lance says. "You must seize the day. Be the best you can at everything you do. Press on and never give up." Really, there's just one major thing that you can learn from this chapter: if you put your mind to something, like Lance did, the sky is truly the limit.

"Money frees you from doing things you dislike. Since I dislike doing nearly everything, money is handy."

-Groucho Marx

The Route to Success!

The Story...

Most people know Michael Dell as the founder of Dell Computers and one of the richest men on the planet. What few people know is that long before he was taking a bite out of Apple, he was sinking his teeth into the business world at the tender age of twelve.

He got a job selling subscriptions to the local paper, and after a while he started seeing a pattern of those who were buying the paper and those who weren't. He saw that there were two groups that were most likely to buy—people who just bought a new home and newlyweds. So he started thinking how he could use this, and an idea popped into his head. He rode his bike down to the courthouse where people register the deeds to their new houses and apply for marriage licenses. He struck gold.

Michael brought together a small army of adolescents that made regular runs to the courthouse pouring through the paperwork looking for leads. Once they had a list of hot prospects, they'd report to Michael and he'd sell. By the end of the summer he was making more than the teachers he was about to be learning from.

The Secret

One of the underlying themes that I've seen throughout writing this book is in just putting two and two together. Instead of wasting his time targeting everyone, he sold to the people most likely to buy.

Also, Michael knew that the information he needed had to be somewhere, so he just did his homework and found the courthouse. I bet Michael wishes there was the Internet when he was a kid—it would have saved him a lot of pedaling.

Now It's Your Turn...

Dell could have looked at his paper job as a dead end like many teens do, but he applied some very grown-up business practices like doing market research and creating a hot list of leads. In the end, he found his business had turned into huge paper profits.

So what's stopping you? I bet you could take just about any job and sell like Dell.

"If you can count your money, you don't have a billion dollars."

-J. Paul Getty

On a Roll!

The Story...

Dominic McVey remembers when he was just eight years old going on trips with his dad and wondering why the men sitting in the front of the plane had nicer seats than the folks sitting in the back. When he learned that you needed to have money to sit in first class, that's when Dominic's entrepreneurial spirit took flight.

All the kids on Dominic's block were crazy about American scooters, but they were hard to come by. So instead of wishing that he had one of these cool scooters, he decided to make it happen. He contacted the company and learned that if he bought five scooters he could get one for free. He knew he would have no trouble selling the other scooters and that he would be able to ride his at no cost at all.

Once those five scooters sold, he discovered that there were another five kids waiting in line, so he ordered more. He kept this cycle going with larger and larger orders each time, and soon he found himself on a wild ride selling 300,000 scooters a week.

As you might imagine, with his business in high gear school took a backseat, but that was okay. To make a long story short, Dominic was honored by the Queen of England for his entrepreneurial skills and has been recognized by the British media as the youngest self-made millionaire in England.

The Secret...

When Dominic decided to go first class, he didn't let anything stop him. How many of us spend our time wishing instead of doing?

Dominic also learned a basic rule of economics: people will pay more for something that's hard to get, and when his friends knew he was able to import scooters, it was all downhill from there.

Now It's Your Turn...

Look around you. What do all your friends want that you can supply? If you can get a toy for $5 and sell it for $10, you've just doubled your money.

Dominic was running an importing business—a very adult thing to do. I'm sure he could've talked himself out of doing it by telling himself, "I'm too young." Instead he kept his eyes on the prize, and the money's been rolling in ever since.

"In the business world, the rearview mirror is always clearer than the windshield."

-Warren Buffett

He's Not Complaining!

The Story...

In most businesses, there's a division where customers can send in a complaint. But at the tender age of fourteen, Ben Casnocha discovered that there was no place on most government sites for feedback. Ben decided to turn this into a class assignment, developing an online complaint form for his local government. His teacher was blown away and encouraged him to take it beyond the classroom. And that's exactly what Ben did.

He started in California and, one by one, governments started adopting his software. By the time he finished high school his software company, Comcate Inc., was a million-dollar company.

Ben is now the author of *My Start-Up Life: What a (Very) Young CEO Learned on His Journey through Silicon Valley* and has been making national headlines on the likes of CNN and the *New York Times*.

The Secret...

Opportunity is knocking all the time, but most kids are too busy listening to their iPods to hear it. Events didn't stop after Ben got an A+ on his project—he saw his product's potential and ran with it.

Go with what you know. Being a software whiz-kid, Ben knew how to make programs, and he turned that knowledge into money. He saw that there was a problem, and whenever there's a problem that needs solving, there's money to be made.

Now It's Your Turn...

You don't have to be a computer know-it-all to know how to make money. What is it that you can do that people will pay you for? Step back, look at what you're good at, and ask yourself, "Is there someone that will pay me for this?" Ben was good with computers, and he's become rich by doing something he'd probably do for free.

Now Ben is the king of online complaints, and he has no complaints at all.

"I don't know the key to success, but the key to failure is trying to please everybody."

-Bill Cosby

The Chair-Man!

The Story...

When Sean Belnick was fourteen years old, he found himself spending a lot of time around his stepdad's office. His stepfather was in the furniture-manufacturing business and sold chairs to furniture stores. Sean could never understand why the furniture store was getting money being the middleman. After all, the furniture store would only place the order with his stepfather, and they would ship the chair to the customer themselves. So he decided to start an internet chair company that he could truly take a stand for.

With a modest investment of $500, Sean started cutting out the middleman, using sites like eBay to sell chairs with very little additional overhead. Soon business began growing rapidly, and he started hiring employees to work under him.

Last year, at the age of nineteen, Sean's company made over twenty-four million dollars through bizchair.com.

The Secret...

Every time you can cut out the middleman, there's money. So think about your own life. Are there times when people are paying retail for something when you can sell it to them wholesale? Often, especially with the Internet, stores are an unnecessary middleman. Anyone who has sold something on eBay understands this: selling something directly to the customer is the way to go.

Now It's Your Turn...

I learned this lesson myself when I was a kid. I used to go to the store to buy my Pokémon cards, but once I stumbled across eBay, I realized things were much cheaper there. Then I started selling the cards on eBay, making handsome profits. After all, I didn't have any overhead. I didn't pay employees; I didn't pay the light bill—just the Internet and shipping, and I was in business.

So what's stopping you? It's time for you to get off of your high chair. You can sit around, or you can be like Sean and take your seat as the chair-man of the board.

"You may be disappointed if you fail, but you are doomed if you don't try."

—Beverly Sills

Making a Splash!

The Story...

When Richie Stachowski was eleven years old, on vacation in Hawaii with his family, he came up with a brilliant idea. He was annoyed that he couldn't talk to his father while snorkeling. He decided to fix the problem by inventing the first underwater walkie-talkie.

Richie was pretty sure with the way kids take to water that this was an idea that would float. So he went on the Internet and started researching designs. When he came up with one he liked, he drained his savings account of $267 to build a prototype. Richie went fishing for retailers, and everyone from Wal-Mart to Toys "R" Us found themselves hooked on his innovative idea.

A few more patents and water toys later, he found himself selling his company for a cool one million dollars. And get this: he was just thirteen years old.

The Secret...

Anyone who says that you're too young is all wet. The secret was that he saw a problem that needed fixing. You can't talk to someone underwater, but like all great inventors, Richie saw an opportunity to invent a way that you could.

He also put his money where his mouth was, he wasn't afraid to pool together his resources and dive in.

Now It's Your Turn...

I'm sure many kids over the years have had the same thought that Richie did: wouldn't it be cool to talk under water? The difference is that Richie acted on it. The next time you find yourself wondering why someone hasn't invented something to solve a problem, think to yourself, "Why shouldn't it be me?"

You don't have to ask me, just ask Richie—it turned out to be the road to riches for him.

**❝Success didn't spoil me,
I've always been insufferable.❞**

-Fran Lebowitz

Bat-Man

The Story...

Have you ever had the feeling that you've forgotten something? Jacob Dunnack, six years old, was having this same feeling when he stepped out of the car upon reaching his grandmother's house. It wasn't long before he realized what he had forgotten—he remembered to bring his baseball bat but left the ball at home.

Rather than simply being disappointed and doing something else, Jacob decided to make sure he never forgot again. Once he got home, he cut out the top of an old, plastic baseball bat and put some balls in it. Then he covered it with Styrofoam so they wouldn't fall out. He knew he had a hit in his hands.

After patenting his new creation, he went straight to his favorite store, Toys "R" Us, and the retail giant instantly saw an out-of-the-park home run. The JD Batball is now sold in over 1,200 Toys "R" Us stores across the United States, establishing Jacob as an MVP in my book.

The Secret...

Jacob knew that he wasn't the only one to ever leave his baseballs at home, but unlike countless of other kids before him, Jacob didn't just see the problem, he saw the solution.

He also knew that coming up with a great idea was just a single. He had a long way to go before reaching home plate. You need to figure out who would manufacture, who would sell, and most importantly you have to act.

Now It's Your Turn...

It's the bottom of the ninth, and you're up to bat. Life is a lot like baseball. You might strike out, but like all great baseball players have discovered, if you can get a hit one out of three times, you can be considered an all-star. How long are you going to ride the bench? Isn't it time to get in the game? Now is the time to batter-up. Step up to the plate and swing for the fences.

"Wealth is the slave of a wise man. The master of a fool."

-Seneca

Chapter Two

PROFIT FROM PASSION

Raising the Chocolate Bar!

The Story...

Lots of kids cook with their grandparents. Elise and Evan Macmillan were no different. From their earliest memories, there was the smell of chocolate in the kitchen as they worked alongside their grandmother to prepare the next cocoa creation. However, this bonding with grandma quickly went from just a pastime into profits when they learned their local bank was putting up a marketplace for kids to sell their goods. So what did Elise and Evan do? They made a beeline to the bank! When the media learned about these mocha moguls, the reporters went crazy. The news stories led to more sales which led to even more news stories, and soon the two found themselves making serious money.

Elise and Evan are now teenage millionaires and have been featured on everything from Oprah to *National Geographic* magazine.

The Secret...

It wasn't just another half-baked idea—their grandma's chocolate had been tested for generations and was always a family hit, but it took their childlike wisdom to see that it could be turned into a business.

If there's one thing children are better at than adults, it's dreaming. When an adult thinks of an idea, they instantly think of all the reasons why it won't work. Children, who haven't been beaten down by the negativity of the world, don't allow themselves to be talked out of their goals.

Now It's Your Turn...

What are your dreams? I'm sure that all of you reading this book are choc-full of ideas, but, whatever you do, don't ever let anyone tell you that your idea won't work. They're your dreams, not anyone else's. Remember, for everyone out there who says something can't be done, there's someone else out there who's already doing it.

So if your parents, your friends, or anyone else tells you that you can't do something, just smile and think to yourself, "Just watch me."

" Fear is that little darkroom where negatives are developed. "

–Michael Pritchard

Pulling a Rabbit
Out of Your Hat!

The Story...

Sterling Dietz saw his first magic show when he was thirteen years old at a local theater, and he instantly knew he had a calling.

"The magician had a table with tricks that you could buy in the back of the room, and I bought everything he had. Three days later, I had my first gig," Sterling jokes. "I got five bucks to do a birthday party."

But to Sterling, that five-dollar bill represented the trick to getting out of manual labor. All his friends in rural Washington picked berries in the fields for ten hours a day.

Now three years later, Sterling is a sophomore in high school, and he travels all over the country doing magic shows for corporate events.

"My best-paying show so far was $2,500." Sterling said in our interview with a smile.

However, Sterling is not greedy—he gives back. He does lots of free shows for worthy causes such as children's hospitals and nonprofits like Boys and Girls Clubs. Sterling knows that the true magic is in sharing your gifts.

The Secret...

Sterling knew that he didn't want to be a berry picker. "My father told me that if you work for someone else, you will never have control over your life. They'll decide when you wake up, where you live, where your kids go to school, everything. But when you work for yourself, you're in control."

Now It's Your Turn...

So what are you waiting for? It's time for you to pull a rabbit out of your hat. Just because all of your friends are doing one thing, it doesn't mean you have to also. Like Sterling, you need to focus on your hocus pocus. Make all of your doubts disappear.

❝Real success is finding your lifework in the work that you love.❞

-David McCullough

Taking Stock of
Your Finances!

The Story...

Just about all kids have played Monopoly and know the feeling of getting rich, even if it's just play money, but Lesley Scorgie decided when she was just ten years old that taking Boardwalk would be a lot more fun in real life.

Instead of reading about the latest teen heartthrob, she began picking up the financial journals and reading about Wall Street windfalls.

Lesley quickly graduated from buying bonds to mutual funds and later to stocks. Her job at the local library kept her plowing money into safe investments.

Her family didn't think much of her interest in money, and none of her friends understood until they saw her on Oprah as a seventeen-year-old financial whiz kid.

Today, she's in her mid-twenties and aims to be worth seven figures by the age of thirty. In fact, she even wrote a book called *Rich by Thirty: A Young Adult's Guide to Financial Success.*

The Secret...

One of Lesley's secrets was delayed gratification. The best thing about bonds and mutual funds is the magic of compound interest—how money can grow by interest. She knew the money would grow all on its own, and when she continued to add to it, her nest egg became a dinosaur egg right out of Jurassic Park!

Now It's Your Turn...

You see your mom and dad reading the business section, looking at the stocks or watching the financial shows on TV—don't automatically think to yourself, "BOR-ING."

Countless fortunes have been made simply by investing in other companies. Just ask Warren Buffet. Before he gave away most of his fortune to charity, he was worth fifty-two billion dollars! If you look on the Top 10 Richest People list, you see mostly people who made stuff. Warren Buffett never made anything other than good investments.

So maybe it's time for you to take stock and bond with the financial section of your paper.

"Keep your face to the sunshine and you cannot see the shadows."

-Helen Keller

The "Write" Stuff!

The Story...

Christopher Paolini was just fifteen years old when he decided to write his first novel. Not unlike J.K. Rowling, he took his childhood fantasies and put them on paper. Little did he know *Eragon* would become a runaway best seller and movie.

The story about a boy and his dragon seemed to strike a chord with legions of fans both young and old. The novel and its sequel have sold more than seven million copies, and the movie grossed a quarter of a billion dollars worldwide. Not bad for a fifteen-year-old, huh?

Christopher is now working on his third book.

The Secret

J.K. Rowling is the richest woman in England for tapping into the vivid imagination of a child, but I bet it's tougher for her than it was for a fifteen-year-old boy who was still living it. Who better to write a story for kids than a kid?

Christopher didn't wait. He took daydreams and turned them into millions of dollars. What would've happened if he had waited? Would he even have been able to recall the colorful figures he had dreamed of when he was a kid?

Now It's Your Turn...

By this point of the book, I'm sure you've seen this theme: all of these child entrepreneurs took action. They didn't wait, they didn't make excuses. They saw an opportunity and tackled it.

There are three kinds of people in this world: those who make things happen, those who watch things happen, and those who say, "What just happened?" Which one are you?

> **"A pessimist sees the difficulty in every opportunity; an optimist sees the opportunity in every difficulty."**
>
> –Sir Winston Churchill

Homeless Hero!

The Story...

Ask any homeless person what the hardest part of being homeless is, and they'll tell you that it's being invisible. No one looks them in the eye because if they make eye contact, they know they'll have to give them money, so everyone pretends they're not there.

Trevor Ferrell remembers seeing homeless people when he was eleven years old, and he couldn't look away. When he saw on the news that it was going to be a "code-blue" night, being so cold that homeless people were being taken off the streets, it sent him over the edge. He knew he had to help.

He had his father take him to a place where homeless people were living, and he gave away one of his blankets. There he saw the devastation that poverty could bring, with thousands of people being left outside at night.

What started with a blanket led to a movement, and he began getting other organizations involved. And when the media learned of it, his story quickly became national news, praising him for having the compassion of Jesus and Ghandi. He was introduced to Mother Teresa and Steven Spielberg. Trevor even got to sit next to Nancy Reagan and was introduced by President Reagan at his 1986 State of the Union address.

If his story sounds familiar, it's because it was made into a book and later a movie.

The Secret...

I include this story as a reminder that success shouldn't just be measured by money. It shouldn't even be the primary motivation—do what you love and the riches will come.

Now It's Your Turn...

What's your purpose? Everyone should strive to leave a mark on the world, to leave the world a better place because you were here. Most of us don't act on our goals because of fear. We're afraid of failure. To paraphrase the great motivational speaker Les Brown, the reason why most people fail is not because they aim too high and miss, it's because they aim too low and hit.

**" If you can DREAM it,
you can DO it. "**

-Walt Disney

Boys Under the Hood!

The Story...

When Robert Lewis Dean was born his parents didn't give him a rattle, they gave him a wrench. It seemed he was always fixing something—Tonka trucks, matchbox cars—if it had wheels, Robert was fixing it.

In fact, he remembers when he was just fifteen years old, he borrowed $1,500 from his parents and bought an old 1972 Cadillac. It took a while, but he fixed it up and sold it at a profit. Robert was so excited about making money doing something he loved that he opened Coach House Cars, an antique-car restoration business, and his cash flow kicked into high gear.

Robert knew he could make big bucks if he concentrated on the classics. He went to work on everything from 1942 Packards to '52 Thunderbirds. He couldn't believe people would pay so much money for something he'd practically do for free.

When he was seventeen years old, he sold the business while it was grossing $600,000 a year.

The Secret...

Robert turned his interest into income by looking at what he loved and figuring out a way to make money off of it. He also recognized the premium that people would pay to purchase their dreams.

The parts that go into a 1957 classic car are worth maybe a few thousand dollars, but a '57 Thunderbird, lovingly restored by an auto artist like Robert, can bring in $60,000.

Now It's Your Turn...

Sometimes to make money you need to get your hands dirty. Most of us go through life with our emergency brakes on—our car is constantly jerking to a stop with thoughts that kill our momentum, like, "I'm too young," or, "Nobody will take me seriously; I'm just a kid." Now is the time for you to take your foot off the brake and step on the gas.

"And in the end, it's not the years in your life that count. It's the life in your years."

-Abraham Lincoln

Rap Sheet!

The Story...

Devin Lazerine has always loved rap music, but when he decided to look for magazines about the rap world, he was at a loss. There was nothing out there talking about the emerging artists and hit songs he loved. So, he figured, who better to capture all of the hip-hop hype than him?

He decided to start a Web site first, and at fifteen years old Devin registered rap-up.com. As word spread on the Internet about his site, he started becoming something of a hip-hop hero and caught the eye of a publisher. That's when he started to think ink.

However, Devin was careful to do all of his business over e-mail or through letters. He knew that it would be a lot harder to be taken seriously if they knew his age.

As rap music gained in popularity, his magazine sales followed, and soon it was climbing up the charts.

Today *Rap-Up Magazine* prints 200,000 copies bimonthly, and Devin is finding himself well on his way to becoming a magazine millionaire.

The Secret...

He was lucky to have been born in the Internet age, because anyone who's googling rap and hip-hop has a chance to find his Web site. When your mom and dad were growing up, their whole world was pretty much their immediate neighborhood. These days, if you have Internet access, the whole world is your candy store.

On the Internet, all you need is a good looking Web site. People won't know if you're a company of 1 or 1,000—you become whatever the visitor wants to believe.

Now It's Your Turn...

If you don't have a Web site, what's stopping you? Whether you have a babysitting business, mow lawns, or even sell lemonade, everyone should have a Web presence.

Stop making excuses. Steven Spielberg says that he doesn't dream at night. He dreams all day.

"The greatest mistake you can make in life is to be continually fearing that you will make one."

-Ellen Hubbard

Not Just
Hanging Around!

The Story...

If you have ever lost a person you loved, you know how devastating it can be. By the time Jena Sims was ten years old, she had lost both of her grandparents to cancer, but rather than just living with the pain of the loss, she focused her energy on something positive.

She developed ornaments dedicated to people who had died from cancer. She began selling them at hospitals for ten dollars each, with the proceeds going to the American Cancer Society (ACS). Customers were so hooked on her ornaments that she could hardly keep up with demand.

Since her start, Jena has made over $80,000 which has been donated to the ACS.

The Secret...

Jena learned at a very early age that there are always set-backs in life that you can't control and pain that you can't avoid, but how you choose to handle these problems is completely up to you. Dwelling on the loss isn't the answer. Instead, she turned her pain into a purpose and found a way to help others heal.

Now It's Your Turn...

"Every teen can do something to make a difference, but I think many don't know where to start. Think about your passions and try to find a way to incorporate those into how you give back to the community. When speaking to community officials, always be professional and prepared to show that you're committed to making a change. Then, when all the hard work of planning and organizing is done, have fun doing your project and be sure to notice how much of a difference you're making!"

Think about any situation where you had pain and think about your reaction to it. Life is just a series of two steps forward and one step back. Once you learn, like Jena, that adversity is a fact of life, you'll discover life isn't about the destination, it's about the journey.

"There are two kinds of people, those that do the work and those that take the credit. Try to be in the first group, there is less competition there."

-Indira Gandhi

Chapter Three

TAKING ACTION

Magazine Queen!

The Story...

Kenya Jordana James remembers when she was eleven years old, going through the magazine racks and being surprised to see that there weren't any for African-American girls. So she started her own. *Blackgirl Magazine* features African-American celebrities and role models and articles that would be interesting to black teens. The bimonthly magazine has allowed her to interview music acts such as Outkast and tennis superstars Venus and Serena Williams. Her unique magazine was an instant hit and has been steadily gaining subscribers. *Blackgirl Magazine* now reaches 4,000 subscribers every two months, giving her close to a six-figure salary.

Her story was quickly picked up by the media, and she was even featured on Oprah.

The Secret...

Kenya saw a void and filled it. Unlike most people who find a need and say to themselves, "Someone should invent this," Kenya went out and did it. She decided that someone had to do it, and it might as well be her.

We all suffer from the same vitamin deficiency: Vitamin A—Action. We know what to do, but we just don't do it. We know that diet and exercise help us lose weight, but we keep getting heavier. Kenya saw a need and acted on it.

Now It's Your Turn...

When was the last time you said to yourself, "Someone should invent ___"? Next time you catch yourself saying someone should do something, be that someone. Kenya clearly had a burning desire. Creating the magazine was something that she had to do. Life is too short—you don't want to wake up one day and look back at your life and ask yourself, "Why didn't I?"

In every survey I've ever seen of people who are near death, the most common regret is that they didn't take more risks.

"We are all manufacturers. Making good, making trouble, or making excuses."

-H.V Adolt

When Life Gives
You Lemons...

The Story...

Just about every kid, at some time or another, has run a lemonade stand. When I was eight years old, my sister and I opened a lemonade stand and got on the six o'clock news! And it wasn't an accident that we opened right in front of the TV station either. Like many kids, however, we didn't make much money, and our interest in sitting around in the hot sun melted away just like the ice cubes in our pitcher.

That's what makes Kyle Orent's accomplishment so impressive. For his seventh birthday this New York boy asked for one thing: a lemonade stand. Young Kyle is a born salesman, and he knew better than to wait for the customers to come to him. He put his lemonade stand on wheels and went to where the customers were: the soccer fields and up and down the business district of his town. Day after day he would quench the thirst of businessmen and women, soccer players, and their parents. However, Kyle didn't blow his dough on the latest video game. This kid was on a canine crusade.

Kyle has always had a soft spot for animals, and when he learned about a group called Canine Companions, it was puppy love at first sight. This organization helps train companion dogs for the disabled. Over the course of the year, Kyle raised $20,000. People weren't just giving him a couple quarters for a cool lemonade—knowing the donations were going to a good cause, people were giving him tens and twenties, and he even got one check for $800.

Who knows what Kyle will use his talents for next? Whatever he decides to do, you can bet that this kid will squeeze every little drop out of life.

The Secret...

It was Kyle's love for animals that gave him such dogged determination on this project. I'm sure there may have been days when Kyle didn't feel like pulling that cart to the soccer fields. It would have been easier to sit at home and play Xbox, but he knew that hitting a new high score wouldn't make a difference like uniting disabled people with a four-legged friend.

Now It's Your Turn...

Who knows how successful I could have been if I had kept my lemonade stand up longer? What if, instead of setting myself up in front of a TV station, I had set up shop in front of a construction site filled with thirsty workers? Instead of sticking with it, I did what most kids do: I moved on. It's up to you whether you want to sell a couple pitchers of lemonade for a pack of Pokémon cards or several thousand pitchers to pay your way through college.

"Perseverance is failing 19 times and succeeding the 20th."

-Julie Andrews

Babysitting Bonanza!

The Story...

When Brenda Elliot was just twelve years old she got her first babysitting job.

"I was making two dollars an hour," Brenda jokes. "And even then that wasn't a lot of money."

But Brenda loved kids, and her passion for Pampers quickly made her the neighborhood nanny. Word of mouth about Brenda's babysitting business kept her booked solid and she didn't stop there. She was always looking for new clients.

"I would actually look at the birth announcements in the paper and send all the new moms a congratulations letter and a flyer, just in case they hadn't already settled on a sitter."

Unlike other girls her age, Brenda didn't blow her dough on the latest Barbie. Brenda's dream was to buy herself a car and to pay her way through college.

"Every time I saw something in the store that I wanted, I started thinking about the car and how much I wanted that more."

The dollars in her savings account began stacking up, and by the time she was finishing high school she had become a real-life nanny making far more than two dollars an hour. She even saved up enough to put $10,000 in her own IRA (Individual Retirement Account). That $10,000 dollars is now $50,000 and is still growing.

The Secret...

Brenda learned at an early age the difference between needs and wants. You need to eat. You don't need an iPod—you want it. Brenda saw the big picture, and she asked herself, "What do I want more—the latest one-hit wonder that'll end up a piece of junk in my closet or a new car that will give me independence?"

Now It's Your Turn...

Brenda suggests that you really stop and think about what your long-term goals are. If it's getting a car, ask your mom and dad to take you down to the car dealership to look at your dream car and see how much you need to save to buy it. Or if you want to go to college, go to your dream school and picture yourself walking around the campus.

"You win some, you lose some, and some get rained out, but you gotta suit up for them all."

-J. Askenberg

Chew on This!

The Story...

Her real name is Kailyn Cage, but since she always seemed to have some candy on her, everyone just called her Candy Girl. So, living up to her name, Kailyn decided to make money off of her reputation by bringing a backpack full of candy to sell to her 7th grade classmates.

Unfortunately, Kailyn soon found out that what she was doing was prohibited and her little business was forced to close up shop. However, by the end of it all, she had made her first $1,000. And rather than stop permanently, she decided to keep going—except this time, legally.

Kailyn invested some of the profit she made her first time around into some candy machines, and after getting permission from some local business owners, she set them up in their stores. She studied what the customers were buying and adapted, changing her supply to the popular demand. With all of this money coming in, it gave her an opportunity to again expand her domain, and soon she found herself on a Tootsie Roll.

She made $10,000 in one year off her candy cache, all while running track and maintaining a high GPA.

The Secret

One of the secrets Kailyn used to get her Payday is that she used her reputation to her advantage. She was already the Candy Girl, so who else was better suited to sell candy to kids in need?

Also, even after the devastation of finding out that her business actually wasn't allowed, she didn't give up. She just found a way to continue legally.

Now It's Your Turn...

We've all heard the song "I Want Candy," right? That's a great example of how most of us kids are. We want candy, we want a video game, and ultimately we want to go to college, but most of us don't follow through with our dreams and find a way to get that candy.

Listen, the reason why I told the story of Kailyn and her business wasn't to feed you, it was to make you hungry. Sink your teeth into whatever market you pursue and never let go.

"If you would be wealthy, think of saving as well as getting."

-Benjamin Franklin

Raking in the CASH!

The Story...

John Shorb was in the 6th grade when he began mowing lawns for his neighbors, and from the start he busied himself with gaining new clients. By the time he entered high school, his list of customers was still getting bigger, and soon he found himself running a highly successful landscaping business.

He would wake up extra early to work on lawns before school, and he even avoided sports to maintain his business. John took his job so seriously that when his family went on vacation, he stayed home in Washington to look after his customers' yards. John's extreme dedication to his work paid off big time. By the time he was nineteen, John had over 120 regular customers and five full-time employees, with total gross income reaching $125,000.

The Secret...

The secret of this story is simple: dedication. When most kids were hitting the snooze button on their alarm, John was out working on his customers' lawns. I know I speak for all of us when I say that missing out on some sleep is about as dedicated as you can get.

Charging to do things that no one else wants to do is a great way to make money. The reason why his business worked so well is that not many people like to mow the lawn or do yard work, so they gladly paid him to do it for them.

Now It's Your Turn...

Tony Robbins once said that the real opportunity for success lies in the person and not in the job. It doesn't matter what you choose to do, as long as you try your hardest and never give up.

If you choose to plant the seeds in your business life now, as a kid, just watch—your success and entrepreneurial spirit will end up growing like weeds. And if you work as hard as John, you'll prove that your business is a cut above the rest.

"Money was never a big motivation for me, except as a way to keep score. The real excitement is playing the game."

-Donald Trump

Gray's Anatomy!

The Story...

His last name is Gray, but there has never been any shade of gray in his business plan. Farrah Gray knew when he was just six years old that he was born to be somebody, and he wasn't going to let his age stop him.

He grew up in inner-city Chicago and had been born into poverty. He remembers sometimes not even having food in the fridge. After a while, Farrah began asking himself why he had to live this way, and he decided that six-years-old was as good a time as any to change it.

So he grabbed some baby lotion and anything he thought he could sell, and began going door-to-door. When he ran out of items he ran home for more to sell. Farrah remembers how wonderful it felt to come home with enough money to treat his mom to Chinese food. He wanted more. And he knew the fortune he was going to achieve wasn't going to be found in any cookie.

Farrah became a serial entrepreneur. It started with a neighborhood investment club in which he raised $15,000. Then he became the co-host of a radio show, and by age twelve he was commanding $10,000 a speech as a nationally known speaker.

However, he kicked all of his success into high gear when he started his own food company based on his grandma's pancake recipe. He called it Farr-Out Foods. Farrah sold the company for one million dollars, making him the youngest self-made African-American in history at the age of fourteen.

The Secret...

For Gray, it was black-and-white: either he went out there and did something or his family went hungry. All great entrepreneurs need some fire in their bellies. You need to be so determined that you will not be denied—because everyone sits back and wishes they were rich. It's the ones who go out and actually do something about it who end up being successful.

Now It's Your Turn...

How hungry are you? For Farrah, it was actual hunger. But what I'm talking about is finding your motivation. Don't dream it, do it. As hockey legend Wayne Gretzky likes to say, "100 percent of the shots you don't take are the ones guaranteed to miss."

"If one advances confidently in the direction of his dreams, and endeavors to live the life which he has imagined, he will meet with success unexpected in common hours."

-Henry David Thoreau

S-no Problem!

The Story...

I think we've all had this annoying problem: we're working on building the ultimate snow fort, and even though we're wearing gloves, that snow keeps finding its way down our sleeves. K-K Gregory, who was ten years old at the time, was experiencing this same thing when she decided to find a way to fix it.

K-K went to work on a solution. With the help of her mom, she sewed together a special detachable sleeve that would block out the snow. When she discovered that other kids wanted some, she applied for a patent and actually started manufacturing them. She decided to call them Wristies.

These Wristies were a major hit in the neighborhood, but her big break came when she made an appearance on the shopping channel QVC. In the first six minutes she made over $22,000.

Since then she's been granted numerous awards and has even appeared on Oprah.

The Secret...

K-K didn't doubt herself—she could've easily written it off as just another flaky idea, but she had the confidence to go forward. She tested it on her friends, applied for a patent, and then actually started to manufacture them. It's been smooth sledding since then.

She also used her age to her advantage. I have no doubt that many of those moms and dads at home watching QVC bought those Wristies not only because it was a clever invention but because a kid had made it. Don't be afraid to use your age to your advantage.

Now It's Your Turn...

What great ideas have you come up with that you never bothered to put down on paper? There are lots of great ideas that never get done. I've always thought that the richest property in any town is the cemetery, because that's where all the unfulfilled dreams were buried.

❝Designing your product for monetization first, and people second will probably leave you with neither.❞

-Tara Hunt

Support
Our Troops!

Girl Scout Cookies...

$4 per box

One Smart Cookie!

The Story...

At the beginning of the year, just about every home gets hit up by an army of pint-sized entrepreneurs, better known as Girl Scouts. Who can say no to a freckle-faced kid holding a clipboard ready to take your order of two boxes of Thin Mints?

Seven-year-old Victoria Rose Meek was one Brownie determined to be the cookie queen. Every afternoon after school for three months she would put on her uniform and open up her cookie stand in her front yard. If her green sign reading "Cookies for $4" didn't get your attention, she had no problem breaking into song singing, "I want cookies, girl scout cookies" to get you to stop by her stand.

On her first day she sold 200 boxes, and that was just the beginning. She had her eyes on the ultimate prize: a helicopter ride over her hometown. Day after day, even in the rain, she would work in the stand. She had a brilliant pitch. Even if you weren't interested in buying the cookies for yourself, she would suggest, "Don't you want to buy some cookies for the troops in Iraq?" taking advantage of the Girl Scouts' "Operation Thin-Mint" program.

She sold a total of 2,006 boxes to take the top prize. For Victoria, it was personal. Her father is in the Navy, and he was there in uniform to watch her with pride as the helicopter took off.

The Secret...

Victoria had a goal. For some people, the goal is money; for others, it's fame. For this seven-year-old, it was all about her dad. She knew that if she could outsell every other Brownie, she'd be able to not only do something good for the troops, she'd also be able to show her stuff in front of her dad.

When it was raining, it would have been very easy for Victoria to come up with plenty of excuses, but she stayed out to sell anyways. She was so focused on the cookie count, she could taste victory.

Now It's Your Turn...

What are your goals? You can't enter a race if you don't know where the finish line is. One entrepreneur I know says he makes a finish line, but once he reaches it, he keeps moving it further away. If you make goals then, like Victoria, you'll find yourself making a thin mint.

**"If you come to a fork
in the road, take it."**

-Yogi Berra

Keeping It Clean!

The Story...

His future looked bright. At the age of fifteen, Barry Minkow started his own carpet cleaning business, called ZZZZ Best, and started cleaning up in every sense of the word. In fact, at one point he was making more than the principal of his high school, and all of his classmates knew it.

As soon as he was able, he took the company public. It made millions as the stock began to rise, and Barry was soaking it in. He bought a mansion, a Ferrari, and started living the easy life.

However, according to published reports, Minkow found himself leading a double life. To the outside world, he was a highly respected and successful teenage entrepreneur who drove a Ferrari, but secretly he was taking money from one investor to pay another, and he found himself in a legal bind.

According to one newspaper, once the bubble had burst on his questionable business practices, all of his credibility dissolved. He was sentenced to twenty-five years in prison.

In prison he turned his life around by becoming a Christian. He now goes around the country warning others not to do what he did and does his part in preventing fraud in other companies.

The Secret...

I saved this chapter for the very end because it's a good lesson in running your business with honesty and integrity. If you work hard, you can achieve anything you want to in this country, but it comes with a catch. You've got to use your entrepreneurial powers for good instead of evil, because what goes around comes around. Barry Minkow had many years in prison to think about that.

Now It's Your Turn...

In his famous speech, Martin Luther King, Jr. dreams of a day when people will be judged by the content of their character. The same goes for you: it doesn't matter about the dollars in your bank account, it's all about your honesty and integrity. There are lots of ways to get rich, but if you can't look yourself in the mirror, it's a very poor reflection on how you're living your life.

"It ain't about how hard ya hit. It's about how hard you can get hit and keep moving forward."

-Rocky Balboa

About the Author

Dallas Crilley...

...is a fifteen-year-old budding entrepreneurial superstar who plans to make his first million dollars selling this book to people like you. Thanks for contributing to his college fund and keeping him out of trouble.

To order extra copies of this book, please send your name, address, and $20.00 (plus $5.00 to cover postage and handling) to my dad's P.O. Box in Texas:

P.O. Box 702606
Dallas, TX 75370

To order extra copies of this book online, go to my Web site. If you have any questions, or if you're interested in booking Dallas to speak, please go to

www.kidpreneurclub.com
or e-mail Dallas at

dallas@kidpreneurclub.com.

Genius Ways For Kids
To Pay Their Way Through College

and its contents are © 2008 Dallas Crilley.